CONTENTS

A WORLD OF FLAGS

Wherever we go in the world, we will see flags. Flags come in different colors, patterns, and sizes. Many flags have symbols or emblems that have special meaning for the people who use them.

There are special flags for cities, towns, states, families, and members of royalty. Sometimes, large business and sporting organizations even have their very own flags.

THE FIRST FLAGS

People have flown flags for more than three thousand years. Vexillologists (people who study and collect information about flags) say that the first flags were called "vexilloids." Vexilloids were made from wooden or metal poles that had carved objects attached to them. Cloth or silk flags, which are similar to the flags we know today, were first made in ancient China.

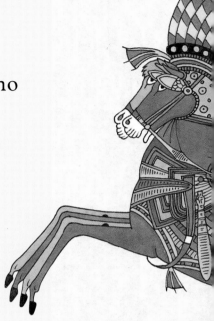

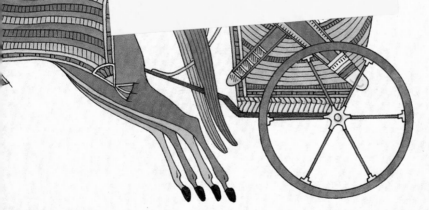

The Egyptians are thought to be the very first people to use flags. They made their flags from objects that represented the gods of the Egyptian world. Soldiers carried these flags into battle, hoping the gods would protect them and bring them victory.

The Romans also carried flags into battle. The armies of the Roman legions, under the ruling caesars, displayed flags in the royal colors.

In ancient China, the emperors of the Zhou dynasty ordered that a white flag announcing their presence must precede them in their travels.

Today

Prime mini
presidents, and
members of royalty
fly flags on their
vehicles to announce
their arrival to the
public.

FLAGS OF CLAN AND FAMILY

Throughout history, people have often flown flags that identify their family, or their allegiances, or loyalties, to groups in society.

In Japan, the flags of the samurai warriors carried family emblems.

Today...

On the fifth of May, many Japanese families follow the tradition of flying fish-shaped flags outside the family home to celebrate the lives of their sons.

In England, flags with pictures of dragons, lions, and other animals flew from the royal houses.

In Scotland, all the clans had flags. These flags flew from the castle turrets or from the walls surrounding the village.

FLAGS OF THE BATTLEFIELD

When an army went into battle, the soldiers carried the flag of their country. The flag was thought to inspire courage in those who fought under it. People often said that soldiers died for their flag and their country.

The Stars and Stripes of the United States of America has its roots in the battlefields of the American Revolution. Many historians believe that Betsy Ross, a Philadelphian seamstress, made the first United States flag and presented it to George Washington. Betsy persuaded the people who designed the flag to replace a six-pointed star with the five-pointed star.

People believed the loss
of the flag in battle meant
almost certain defeat, so
the flag bearer was always
protected by surrounding
soldiers.

When an army faced
defeat, soldiers would
sometimes wave a white
flag to signal their
surrender. This is
because soldiers carrying
a white flag were not
supposed to be shot at.
(White flags were often
made from torn shirts,
as no army was
prepared to lose.)

Regimental flags are called "colors." In a time when many soldiers could not read or write, the colors were used to help soldiers pinpoint their regiment's location in a battle. The regimental colors were always paraded (or trooped) through the ranks once a week so that they would be set in the memories of the soldiers.

Today...

In Great Britain, people from all over the world gather to watch the "Trooping of the Colours" ceremony held every June.

FLAGS OF VICTORY

People all over the world fly flags to announce that a special event or some great achievement has taken place.

In 1953, New Zealander Sir Edmund Hillary and Nepalese Sherpa tribesperson Tensing Norgay became the first people to reach the top of Mt. Everest. Their flags flew from the top of the highest place in the world to claim victory in climbing the mountain.

Norwegian explorer Roald Amundsen was the first person to plant a flag in the coldest place on Earth: the South Pole.

When British explorer Captain Robert F. Scott reached the Pole a month later, he found the victorious Norwegian flag still flying.

As far back as 1492, Christopher Columbus flew a Spanish flag from a flagpole in the Americas – a new land he claimed to have discovered.

In July 1969, when Neil Armstrong and Edwin (Buzz) Aldrin walked on the moon, they flew the Stars and Stripes. The flag told the TV-watching world that the United States of America was the first nation to successfully land astronauts on the moon.

Today...

People wave flags at parades to acknowledge special achievements and to celebrate the return of heroes.

MESSAGES IN FLAGS

In the past, people used flags to send messages to one another. Even today, people all around the world use flags to communicate.

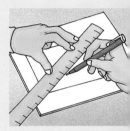

The flags in this picture tell swimmers: Swim here! This area is safe for swimming.

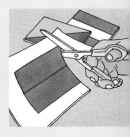

When motor cars first started sharing the road with other travelers, many people thought the cars were too dangerous. People were employed to walk in front of cars and wave red flags to warn that a motor car was coming.

People use the international flag code to send messages to one another. Each special flag stands for a letter of the alphabet.

You can copy the flags from this international flag code to send messages to your friends.

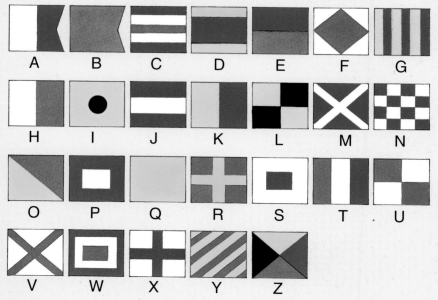

Flags can warn ship crews that bad weather is approaching.

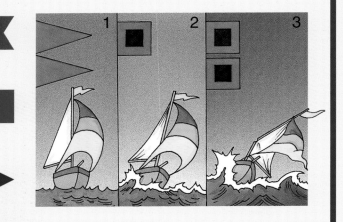

1   Gale Warning:
    Wind speeds of
    32 to 63 miles per hour

2   Storm Warning:
    Wind speeds of
    64 to 73 miles per hour

3   Hurricane Warning:
    Wind speeds over
    74 miles per hour

In many countries, when someone dies, flags are flown at half-mast as a sign of respect.

Semaphore flags were used to convey messages between ships at sea. The signaler held two flags in various positions to "spell out" a message.

K E E P

A W A Y

FLAGS IN SPORTS

In the world of sports, people use flags to communicate directions or warnings.

In soccer, linespeople wave flags to tell the referee where the ball went out of play.

In auto racing, a black-and-white checkered flag is used to tell drivers that they have crossed the finish line. Flags are also flown to signal everything from "look out for oil on the track" to "look out – accident ahead."

In slalom events, skiers must be able to zigzag at high speeds between a series of flags, called "gates."

Flags tell cross-country riders how to approach a fence – the red flag is on the rider's right.

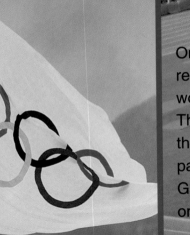

One of the most recognized flags in the world is the Olympic flag. This flag symbolizes the unity of countries participating in the Olympic Games, which are held once every four years.

Did you know...

The world's biggest flag was made for the 1992 Olympic Games, which took place in Barcelona. It weighed nearly 1,800 pounds.

FLAGS AROUND THE WORLD

Many people give the flags of their countries special names. People often have strong feelings about their national flag.

The flags of both New Zealand (left) and Australia (right) feature the stars of the Southern Cross.

The flag of Switzerland has a white cross on it.

Some states in the United States have animals on their flags. California has a bear, and Wyoming has a buffalo.

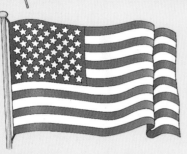

The people of America call their country's flag the Stars and Stripes.

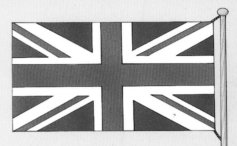

The people of Great Britain sometimes call their flag the Union Jack.

The flag of New Guinea has the bird of paradise on it.

The flag of Canada has a maple leaf on it.

INDEX

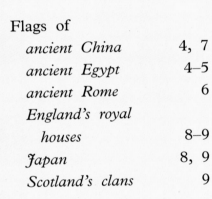

ABOUT STEVE PATTRICK

 Steve Pattrick is an Australian author who loves writing for children. When he is not writing, he spends his time teaching children's theater or going to the movies.

Steve says that his fascination for flags arose from his childhood interest in military history and the flags that flew on various battlefields.

When he is writing a new book, Steve drives to a remote beach cottage and curls up with Bobby, his cat, and his computer. Steve says, however, that he is sure "the cat is more interested in the computer mouse" than his stories.

Written by **Steve Pattrick**
Illustrated by **Kelvin Hawley**
Edited by **Sue Ledington**
Designed by **Kristie Rogers**
Photographic research by **Sarah Irvine**

Photography by **Key-Light Image Library:** (p. 7); **N.Z. Herald:** (Olympic flag in stadium, p. 27); **N.Z. Picture Library:** (pp. 12-13; pp. 14-15; Moon walk, 1969, pp. 16-17; Olympic flag, p. 26); **Photobank Image Library:** (cover; p. 9; parade, p. 17; p. 18; Olympic opening ceremony, pp. 26-27); **Photosport:** (pp. 2-3; p. 25; pp. 22-24; woman holding American flag, p. 27)

05 04 03 02 01
10 9 8 7 6 5 4

Distributed in the United States of America by
Rigby
a division of Reed Elsevier Inc.
1000 Hart Road
Barrington, IL 60010

Printed in Hong Kong through Colorcraft Ltd
ISBN: 0-7901-1680-4